Naval Heritage in the West

by Andy Endacott

PART III

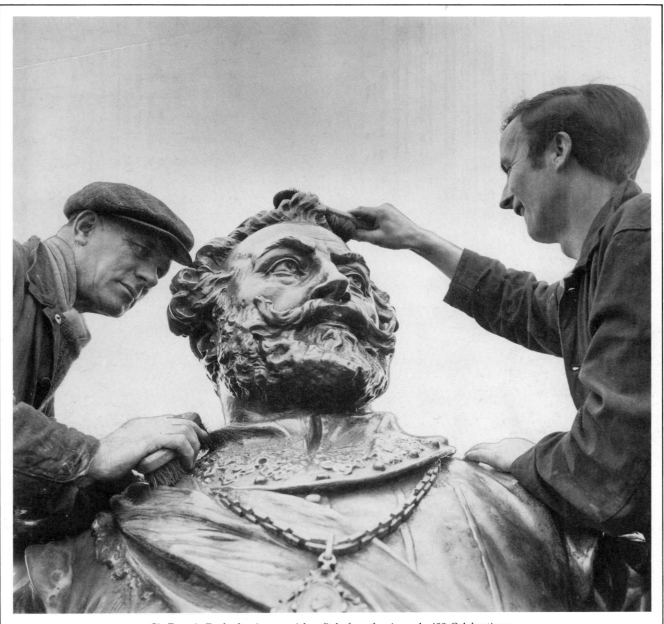

— Sir Francis Drake having a quick refit before the Armada 400 Celebrations. —

Three generations of Naval Heritage—HM King George V, HM King Edward VII and the Duke of Cornwall, circa 1908.

Available from bookshops, other titles in this series:

Naval Heritage in the West Part I 1800—1910
Covers the early building of the Dockyard, the wooden wallers, shore training schools, gunnery, coaling ship and activities on the River Tamar.

Naval Heritage in the West Part II 1900—1950
The battleship era, shipbuilding, early submarines, Colleges, Fleet Air Arm, WRNS, Royal Marines and local items on and adjacent to the River Tamar.

ISBN *0.9511527.2.6*
First published: *June 1988*
Text © D.L. ENDACOTT 1988

Published by D.L. ENDACOTT, 58 GLENHOLT ROAD, PLYMOUTH, and printed by Penwell Ltd., Parkwood, Callington, Cornwall.

INTRODUCTION

This, the third part, will complete my brief glances at our Naval Heritage. As the books have progressed, more and more information has been offered from readers, tempting the production of booklets on many branches of the system, and already I have included a 'flash-back' group of pictures following many readers' requests. Those of you who will be around in the 21st Century, with space travel, computers and hi-tech weapon systems, will hopefully be able to recall the old days via collections such as these.

In this volume we see the end of shipbuilding in the Yard and the big ships, guns and traditions passing into history. Post-War development and continuing improvements in design gave the Navy the helicopters of today which are carried by most ships and used by land forces and civilian Rescue Groups alike.

The Royal Marines have become a formidable Commando force, ready to spearhead any action, as demonstrated in the Falklands campaign. The WRNS, now in their 70th year, have also come a long way and acquired high skills, thus releasing the men for other specialist work. Additional training establishments have been created and the WRNS have moved down to HMS Raleigh. The map on the inside of the back cover shows the wealth of facilities in the West Country today, of which we should be very proud.

In 1929 the Dockyard was very worried about its future, but it survived and expanded. Again, in 1987/88 there is cause for concern, with a reduced Navy, a smaller repair programme and the upheaval of new commercial management, but I am sure that with its great capabilities the Yard will still be a force to be reckoned with in the years ahead.

No review of our naval heritage would be complete without a mention of those establishments which daily ''serve the Crown'' and also the civilian manned RFA's which are the Navy's lifeline.

The wooden hulled sail-ship of 1588 and the sea-faring activities of Drake are a long way from the 20th Century naval cylindrical-shaped vessel called a nuclear submarine, which moves underwater, can operate indefinitely from that position and poses a great threat to a potential enemy. Let us hope that it is never necessary in the future to bring any of our ultra-modern developments into a real battle situation.

So—reflect back over the three volumes of Naval Heritage in the West and the good old days of Naval traditions, the British Empire and supporting cast from all walks of life. As long as the content has aroused sufficient interest, I shall feel that the research and collation have been well worth while.

Acknowledgements:

In compiling these books, much help has been needed, and I would like to thank the following for their support—the PROs at Britannia, Cambridge, Culdrose, Lympstone and Mount Wise for Crown Copyright sources: Central Photos, the Naval Hospital and the Naval Base Photo Section, Sea Cadet Corps and AVA Torpoint.

Help from private sources was also invaluable—from the late B. Best, G. Brooks, J. Broad, C. Gill, the late J. Kingston, K. Hemsil, Mrs K. Lock, J. Makin, D. Northcott, Mrs J. Perkins, Mrs S. Paddon, M. Parsons, H. Ross, P. Rowse, R. Skinner, T. Shirley, M. Stevenson, M. Sinclair, C. Trethewey, M. Ware, R. Williamson, Miss Williams and R. Wiltshire. Thanks are due also to the Royal Marine V/C Corps for their help towards an idea that didn't unfortunately reach the drawing board.

Special thanks go to P. Mitchell as my technical proof reader and to Syd Goodman, whose endless help with information and photographs made a large area of this series possible. The unsung heroine of them all is my wife, Marilyn, who has endured the trail of Antique Shops and Naval Book Sales and listened to endless lectures on the Royal Navy, in addition to wading through the minefield of my English Grammar to convert it into the hopefully informative text that you have read. Now the task is completed it must seem to her like the end of a Naval engagement!

Fore Street Gate in 1953, the main gate to the Southern end of the Dockyard, which contained the Building Slips, Plate Shops, Scrieve Board, etc. Shown here with the decorative canopy for Coronation Year. This gate is now well inside the new boundary of the Yard.

END OF AN ERA

HMS Scylla, ''Leander'' Class G.P. Frigate, 2,450 tons, launched 1968. The last frigate to be built in Devonport Dockyard. Shown here having a 35.25 ton unit transferred from the building cradle to the actual slipway for connection.

This was the first time that ships engines, and boilers 33 tons, (shown here) were fitted to any ship on the shipway prior to launching. Because of this additional weight the ''Setting Up Ship'' procedure took a little longer.

The 21 ton weldment of the bow being lowered into position. This section of the ship was to be well used in its career, especially in 1973, when it collided with the Torpoint Ferry on the River Tamar, and when it rammed an Icelandic gunboat *Aegis* during the ''Cod War'' off Iceland.

''Setting up Ship''. This procedure was carried out days before the actual launch. Wedges were driven simultaneously under the cradles, to lift the ship's weight from centre line blocks on to the sliding ways and the CL building blocks were then removed. The ship would be held on the slipway by the trigger mechanism and 4 sets of dog shores.

HMS Salisbury—A/D Frigate, 2,170 tons, launched 1953. The first warship built at Devonport after the second World War, and also the first all-welded construction, on a prefabrication principle. After a much travelled career, she was laid up at Chatham in 1978, and later towed to Devonport as a Training Ship for new-entry recruits at HMS Raleigh. Her final journey in 1985 was to the Northern Approaches, where she was used as a target for bombs and missiles delivered by RAF aircraft.

Holland No. 1, launched in 1901 at Barrow-in-Furness. After serving the Navy she was sold for scrap in 1913 and sank near the Eddystone Lighthouse whilst on tow to the breakers. She lay on the seabed for 69 years until discovered by a local diver and was finally raised by the Admiralty in 1982. We see her here in a dry dock at Devonport, being cleaned externally prior to a preservative being applied to prevent further deterioration from exposure to the air. She is now in the Submarine Museum at Gosport for public viewing.

CRANAGE

These sheer legs built in 1898 on the east side of No. 3 Basin were finally cut down in the mid 1950's and are shown here about to drop into the water. The other set on the west side had been removed in 1915. Mobile steam cranage on railway lines served most docksides from then onwards.

Crane Lighter No. 10—a familiar sight around the Port of Plymouth confines for the last forty-six years. Apart from dockyard personnel not many know about her or the type of work she carries out. Built in 1941 and displacing 920 tons CL 10 has carried out many varied jobs over the years. From serving battleships to survey vessels, perhaps the job she was best known for was that of lifting the Flossies (see page 20) on to the decks of *Eagle* and *Ark Royal* whilst undergoing catapult tests in the Hamoaze.

COMPLEXES

The Central Office Block, overlooking the three Docks, in 1960. The left-hand Dock was for destroyers, and the others for submarines, etc. (see Book 1 page 11). F56—*Argonaut*, is berthed beside the Battery Shop. To the left of the basin is a caisson which allowed ships to be transferred through to the adjacent Basin. The dockside projection inboard from the main caisson entrance created an additional berth, called South Lock, where ships were breast shored so that a Tilt Test check could be made prior to gunnery alignment work.

Frigate Complex opened in 1977 by Dr David Owen. Built over the newly reconstructed 5, 6 and 7 docks, this complex is the biggest of its kind in Western Europe. It allows for continuous working in controlled conditions, and was to assist Devonport in becoming the leading Yard for Leander Class, Type 21 and Type 22 Frigates. Note the slim Tower Cranage on the sea wall.

This high vantage viewpoint shows the Royal Yacht *Britannia* in 1987, being brought out of the Frigate Complex (the Sheds) after having a complete refit, including new teak decking throughout and a complete strip down and repaint of the white superstructure and the hull in its traditional blue. She will soon be earning money for Britain as the world's most exclusive conference centre and a floating showroom for UK exports, in addition to her role as the Royal Yacht.

The Royal Yacht seen moving down the river past the Dockyard on a visit in 1967—note the Reynolds tugs moored in the foreground.

The Submarine Refit Complex was officially opened by HRH the Prince of Wales in 1980 and is situated in the North West corner of the Prince of Wales Basin (No. 5) which was itself opened in 1907 by his great-grandfather. It consists of two dry docks, primarily for SSN refitting, but could be used by frigates if its programme allowed. Dominating the Complex is the 80 Tonne cantilever crane and surrounding its base are control offices and R.U. Workshops. The 9-storey building accommodates both naval and civilian management.

HMS *Defiance*, the fleet maintenance Base, opened by the Prime Minister in 1978, at the top end of the Dockyard adjacent to the S.R.C. Naval officers and ratings are employed on maintenance work in support of ships, submarines and small craft in Devonport and other ports. In the background is Yonderberry Jetty and the town of Torpoint.

MODEL WORK

His Royal Highness is being shown over the model of the SRC, and the modeller has removed sections of the building so that the Prince of Wales can see marked out the route that he will be taking as part of the official opening ceremony.

Since 1694 the Dockyard has built 367 ships of all types for the Navy. The Yard's talents are further portrayed when the modeller produces instructional 1/100th scale ship models, such as the T22 Broadsword seen here, for other establishments at Manadon and Dartmouth College, to serve as detailed training aids for Naval personnel.

A 1/35th scale model of the Main Gate Complex at the R.M. Barracks, Stonehouse. This is the work of J. Makin, a Dockyard employee. He has made the original 'masters' of the various types of model soldiers and cast more using fibre glass. His final superb touch is the hand-painting to complete this "on Parade" scene. Note the two WRNS watrching the event.

As part of the young shipwright's apprenticeship in 1961 he spent a period of time boat-building in his second year. The standard design was the 14ft clinker built sailing dinghy. This construction involved the task of using copper rivets throughout and the steaming of certain timbers to maintain the form.

BIG SHIPS

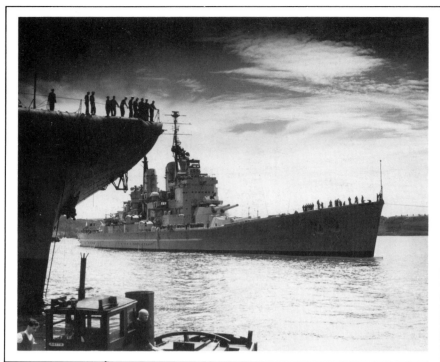

HMS Vanguard coming alongside at the North Yard berth. She was the largest battleship ever built in Britain (Clydebank 1941-46) with a displacement of 50,000 tons fully laden. She never used her guns (15-inch and 5-inch) in anger, and was broken up in 1960.

The Royal Marine Royal Guard on return from the Royal Tour, posing for a photograph on the quarterdeck of HMS *Vanguard*. In the background to the right is the RM Divisional Band.

HMS Nigeria. Launched in 1939, she was a Colony Class cruiser which took part in many operations during the Second World War. Paid off into reserve in 1951, she is pictured here moored off Torpoint where she lay until sold to the Indian Navy in 1957. After refit she commissioned as the *INS Mysore* and continued in service as a Training Ship until 1975.

Attention on the Upper Deck! Seen here on the fo'c'sle of *HMS Duke of York* are almost the entire crew of 1900 men who are blotting out the quadruple and twin 14-inch gun turrets. Whilst in Tokyo it was quoted in September 1945 in ''The Daily Yorker'', the journal of the ship, by Captain Nicholl CBE, DSO—'when we have got the Japs where we want them, my dearest wish will be to sail with this ship and this company into PLYMOUTH SOUND'. This did happen on 11 July 1946, after a global activity of 58,413 miles since leaving Liverpool in April 1945.

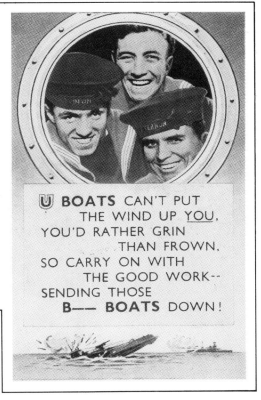

Ⓤ BOATS CAN'T PUT THE WIND UP <u>YOU</u>, YOU'D RATHER GRIN THAN FROWN, SO CARRY ON WITH THE GOOD WORK—SENDING THOSE B—— BOATS DOWN !

LITTLE & LARGE

The first X-craft was built in 1941 and these four-man midget submarines were towed near to the target area by standard submarines and then left to attack by laying delayed action mines. (The most celebrated action was the damaging of the *Tirpitz* German battleship in 1943).

Over 30 warships and auxiliaries can be seen in this aerial view of 'North Yard' in 1964, when the Dockyard and Navy worked together to keep a substantial presence on the high seas. At top right of the picture can be seen the hutted accommodation of the WRNS, known locally as 'HMS Impregnable'. Note the ships—*Bulwark, Hermes, Eagle* and *Ark Royal, Blake, Belfast* and *Roberts, Zeebrugge, Tenacious, Resurgent, Adamant, Tyne, Matapan, Urania, Petard, Sluys* and *Daring.*

WORK HORSES AFLOAT

HM Tug *Pert* as she steamed in and out of Plymouth Sound shepherding her charges. Built by Thornycroft and launched in 1916, she displaced 1,023 tons. Machinery was a Paddle Reciprocating Engine —IHP 2,000—13 knots. She, like *Camel* was sold in 1962 for breaking up. These were not the last paddle tugs to serve at Devonport, as the *Faithful* and *Favourite* were to come into service, though their life spans were shorter than the *Pert* due to the demise of the conventional aircraft carrier, which they were designed to assist when in port.

Until 1972, these commercial tugs owned by W.R. Reynolds of Torpoint, were seen either moored off Torpoint, adjacent to the ferry landing, as shown, or manoeuvring barges up and down the river. The first tug is *Antony*, followed by *Tactful* and *Trevol*, and hidden behind *Antony* is *Carbeil*. These steam vessels were also engaged in Admiralty dumping, service runs to the Eddystone Lighthouse and sludge-carrying operations. They have been replaced by a fleet of diesel tugs. *Antony* and *Trevol* were built by Cox and Co of Falmouth in 1921.

For many years a regular at Devonport Dockyard, the *Camel* served the fleet as a dockyard service tug. Built by Bow McLachlan and launched on 19.10.1914 she displaced 690 tons 144ft (pp) 150.9ft (oa) x 27ft x 11ft, her machinery was a Paddle Reciprocating engine—IHP 1,250 - 12 knots. Seen here with assistance manoeuvring *HMS Unicorn* alongside the Coal Heap at North Yard. She served until 1962 when she was sold for breaking up. Even at this time her engine room was a gleaming brass and copper sight to behold.

Here we can see the RMAS tugs *Robust* and *Rollicker* which were principally built for salvage and long-range towage, manoeuvring *HMS Eagle* past Mount Wise for the last time in 1978 to commence the long journey to the breakers yard at Cairn Ryan, Wigtownshire.

The single screw tug *Typhoon*, built in 1959 for ocean-towing and salvage, shown here in 1970 in her RFA colours of grey and black while operating in the Singapore area. In 1971 she transferred to the RMAS and changed her colour to black and yellow. She was one of the first ships from England to arrive ahead of the main Task Force for the Falklands, spending her time there supplying fresh water, moving troops and towing damaged vessels to safety. Now, in 1987, she is on 14-day Standby Station at Portsmouth.

The Ministry of Defence Police was established in 1971 and in 1975 women were also recruited. They provide a 24-hour policing service throughout the year. Water Police, shown here, play an important role on the River Tamar, covering the ships moored in the area and the frontage of all the Government properties.

FLYING LADIES

This is a wheeled floating Deadload, used to simulate various types of aircraft which the steam catapult on the flight deck would have to launch. *Jane*, pictured here, was one of a group with *Lulu, Lena, Enid* and *Jill*, who were locally referred to as the ''Flossies''. The wire strop below the letters AN actually looped around the sliding shuttle, and overall dimensions were length 19ft, width 14ft and height 7ft.

The impact splash as one of the ''Flossies'' is fired from *HMS Ark Royal* in 1970 at 5/6 Wharf. This demonstrates the need for the MOD Water Police to keep the area well clear during trials. The weight range was 48,000 lbs to 58,000 lbs at speeds of 120 knots and 115 knots respectively.

LEAVING HARBOUR

Approximately 80 years on from the first naval submarines (see page 51 Book 2) the Naval Dockyard now has the capability of handling refit and repair of these large nuclear submarines in the new Complex (see top page 11), one of which is seen here passing the Cremyll slipway. Behind the point the wooden waller *Impregnable* used to berth (see pages 6, 13, Book 1).

MY SWEETHEART AT DEVONPORT

The Telephone Girl has one on every wire.

Leaving harbour and traditionally passing under the watchful eye of Mount Wise HQ (see pages 42, 43, Book 1) at the start of a journey to show the flag in other parts of the world. Thoughts of home and families increase with the passage of time and vital contacts are made possible by telephone and satellite links.

RIVER FERRIES

A ferry service has been operating from Saltash to St Budeaux since 1270 and a steam floating bridge operated from 1850 until 1961. This picture shows the ferry on its final day in 1961. Thereafter all traffic travelled on the new road bridge seen here behind Brunel's famous rail bridge. Naval Base and *HMS Drake* personnel living across the water can no longer experience the early morning journey on the River Tamar.

The ferry service from Devonport to Torpoint has recently had all three ferries lengthened to cope with the increase in traffic. For the new Navy entrant on his or her way to *HMS Raleigh*, crossing this wide stretch of water could in some cases be their first experience afloat since leaving home. Whilst crossing they can glance along the full length of the Naval Base to see many visiting warships.

ROYAL MARINES

A passing-out parade during the Second World War at the RM Infantry Training Centre, Dalditch. Most of the concrete areas are now covered by undergrowth, but a few buildings are still standing to remind any old 'Royals' of their early days in the Hell Hole called Dalditch. Vegetables for these young Marines were obtained at local villages, bread from Exmouth, meat from Exeter, and a weekly convoy collected all bulk dry stores from Plymouth Royal Victualling Yard.

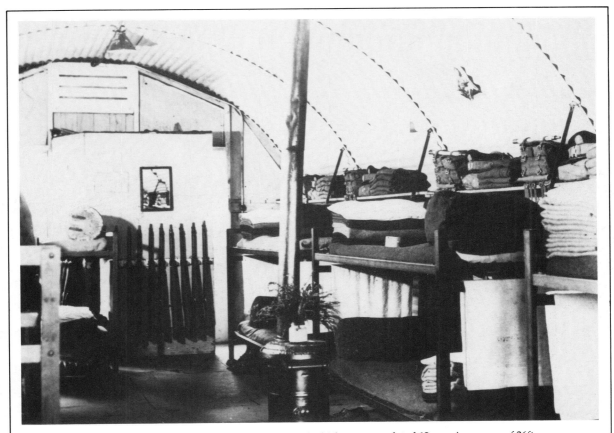

Inside a semi-circular corrugated 'Nissen Hut' which accommodated 12 men in an area of 36ft x 16ft. At Dalditch there were over 300 of these huts on East Budleigh Common during the period 1941 to 1946. Old Royals will recall the rust-covered sides, running wet with condensation, and the aroma of the coke burning circular stove in the centre. (Note the rifle rack secured to the inside of the black-out partition behind the main entrance.)

Weekly fatigues, heaving coal and peeling mountains of spuds, were the just rewards for not paying attention or a possible AWOL punishment, to maintain early discipline.

To encourage the new recruits into developing as efficient and fast operators of equipment, occasional competitions were arranged as shown here —carrying out Bren Gun handling under the watchful eye of the NCO and timekeeper.

The 2nd Sea Lord, Admiral Sir Richard Fitch, KCB, inspecting the Kings Squad of Royal Marines (the Sea Soldiers of the Navy) at Lympstone Training Centre in 1986.

The Princess Royal, who is Chief Commandant of the WRNS, talking to a Wren Royal Marine of the M/T Section during her visit to Lympstone Commando Training Centre in 1980.

RANGE OF DESIGNS

In what appears to be something of a 'Time Warp', the Italian Cadet Training ship *Amerigo-Vespucci* passing through Plymouth waters with men manning the yards, in the late 1970's. This beautiful wooden-waller, capable of carrying 250 cadets, was making a courtesy visit as part of a European cruise.

In 1975, Devonport Dockyard built the largest aluminium mould in the UK (200ft in length). This ship's hull mould was transported to Vospers of Southampton, where a glass-reinforced plastic hull including decks, framing and bulkheads, was made to form the HUNT Class mine countermeasures vessel. Known in many areas as the 'Tupperware Navy', this is a squadron of hi-tech plastic hulled warships. Here we see *HMS Cottesmore* leaving Plymouth Sound in 1984.

With the phasing out of the big Carriers and their jet aircraft, a new breed of ships was required and thus the through deck cruiser was built and launched in 1977; she was the largest warship built for the Royal Navy since the 1950's and was named *Invincible*, with a further two vessels to come at a later period. Capable of carrying Sea King helicopters and the new vertical take-off Sea Harrier aircraft, she is also used for moving troops, as illustrated here on leaving Devonport in 1985. (Note: half the size and complement of *HMS Eagle*).

Endurance, purchased from Denmark in 1967, is painted bright red, to enable her to stand out easily whilst serving her six-monthly duty in the South Atlantic and Antarctic waters. She is fitted with strengthened bow for use in ice, has hydrographic and oceanographic survey capabilities, and watches over British interests in that area—as the Falklands incident was to prove. Shown here leaving Devonport in 1987 after a refit.

TRADITIONS

LAMB'S NAVY RUM

Rum was first issued in the Navy in 1655 as a palliative for poor food and water at sea. In 1824 the daily ration of rum to each sailor was ½ pint. It was later diluted and became known as 'Grog'—after the nickname of Admiral Vernon, 'Old Grogram', who ordered the change.

The last issue of rum was made on 30th July 1970, as pictured here on board *HMS Ark Royal*, by which time it had been reduced to one-eighth of a pint per day. Note: British Navy Pusser's Rum has just been made available to the public, so the tradition can now live on with everyone.

FAMILIES

When the name 'Williams' was mentioned at HMS Raleigh in 1942, clarification was essential as to which Williams you required—CPO Henry or PO Maurice Williams, his son. Henry joined the Navy in 1904 and served on the square-rigged and steam *Northampton*, and Maurice joined Greenwich School at 11 and went to sea at 15 on the Queen Elizabeth. CPO Williams also had a daughter who was a CPO in the WRNS and served from 1940 to 1962, and a younger son who was an AB somewhere at sea when this picture was taken in 1942.

Looking after Maritime personnel and their families is a never-ending task undertaken by KGFS, an organisation well respected by those in or out of the service. It is comforting to know that someone, somewhere, does care and gives help to those who have served their fellow-countrymen so well.

The Royal Fleet Club, built in 1900 at Devonport, with rooms overlooking the Dockyard. It was constructed for the benefit of Sailors and Royal Marines and has family rooms, a lounge and ballroom, where ships' dances, meetings and wedding receptions can be held.

SERVING THE CROWN

Over three generations of dairymen called Tincler & Son have supplied to ships, Messes, Dockyard Canteens and other buildings from this Albert Road Dairy—shown here in 1987 with father and son loading their van.

A little further up Albert Road, Devonport, is another family who have served the Crown, delivering newspapers and periodicals to ships and Dockyard offices. They also cater for employees requiring sweets, cards, etc in the early morning and lunch-breaks and Mrs. Howard is seen here topping up the newspaper rack.

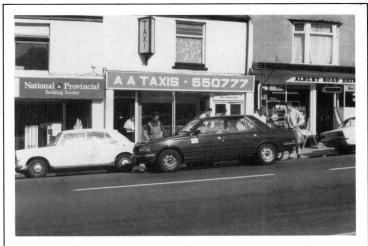

An Albert Road private hire fleet of taxis which has been serving the Dockyard and the ships for 25 years. Here we see "Jack going ashore" (nowadays in civvies) outside the office. The taxis do go into the Dockyard to the brow of a ship when requested, to pick up their Naval fares.

In the late 1950's when "Jack" was finally allowed to go ashore in civvies, this opened the way for Naval outfitters to supply to ships. Their agents were allowed aboard into a messdeck where a range of goods was displayed. Such names as Blooms, Bernards, Cooper, Greenburgh and Louis and Blair (shown here) have kept the fleet supplied. Possibly due to the growth of multiple stores and credit firms, the trading practice has been much reduced in recent years.

From this small shop in Union Street, over 125 years of naval and civilian trading has taken place to all parts of the Globe where the British flag flies. Originally established by the Bindon family, ownership of the shop transferred to Joe Feneck after the War. The firm still supplies tailor-made and off-the-peg clothes and Joe himself has become a listening service and communication link for servicemen who pass through his doors.

PUBLIC PLACES

When the Dockyard expanded from Albert Road, it closed off the through road access from St Levans to Marlborough Street, Devonport, via William Street. This view, in 1966, shows the early building of the large office block, COB1, and the existing church. The temporary single-storey offices were later removed to make a car park area.

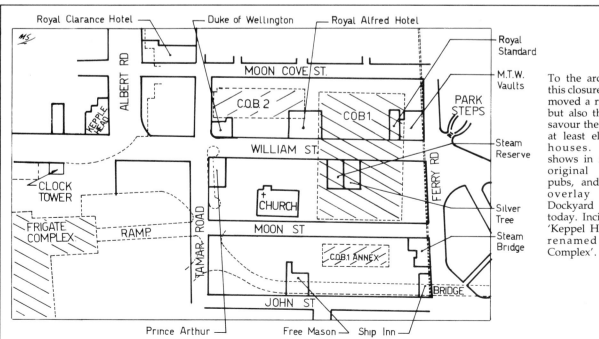

To the ardent drinker this closure not only removed a right of way, but also the facility to savour the drinks from at least eleven public houses. The map shows in full line the original roads and pubs, and the dotted overlay indicates Dockyard buildings of today. Incidentally the 'Keppel Head' is now renamed 'The Complex'.

This public house is situated outside St Levans Gate entrance to the Naval Dockyard. Has a great collection of naval photographs and badges and gives a warm welcome to all during the Navy Day weekend.

TRANSPORT

The passenger train service (see Book 2 page 49) was discontinued in 1966, to be replaced by buses. The last goods train emerged from the tunnel from South to North Yard in 1982 and is pictured here. On that occasion the Port Admiral received from the driver the key token, which had been carried on each journey to ensure that only one train was in the 946 yard long tunnel.

A Dockyard bus passenger service was started in late 1969 and 6 of these Bristol K5G double-decker buses (ex Western National) were used—4 for the Dockyard and 2 for the Navy. The bus shown is ex Western National 995. The fleet was later replaced by Leyland Atlantean double-deckers. During 1984 the double-deckers were replaced by a fleet of Leyland Leopard single-decker 56 seat coaches, which still give a daily bus service over the 2¼ mile length of the Yard at 10 minute intervals.

The starlings literally invade the Dockyard in the Autumn and swarm in their thousands to perch wing to wing along all the tower cranes and similar iron structures. The noise is incredible and working underneath can be hazardous—as depicted in this cartoon.

The vast area of the Dockyard is the territory of these Traffic Wardens. The dockyard has its parking problems—double yellow lines, pedestrian crossings and a shortage of car parks—just like a small town, and the Wardens were introduced in 1971 to ensure compliance with the parking regulations. As a result of their reports parking permits can be withdrawn temporarily or permanently, dependent on the offence committed. Unfortunately, they have no control over the starlings.

"Vicarage Gardens" Camp site 1925 near Saltash Bridge. A shore camp to train cooks, stokers, writers, etc, under the control of HMS Vivid (RN Barracks) and locally called "White City". The buildings on the right hand side of the skyline are the houses and chapel in Normandy Way. In 1928, when the camp was finished, a red-brick Dockyard housing estate was built on the site and still exists, surrounded by other houses.

These four ratings are standing proudly around a trophy won for Parade Ground Drill—an incentive created to produce good keen ratings at the St Budeaux Barracks in 1932. St Budeaux camp overlooked the Coal Heap in North Yard and the WRNS Quarters and is now covered by houses in Furze Park and Roope Close, Barne Barton Estate. The uniforms are No. 5's, a coarse white drill working and washable rig. Apparently residents in Saltash Road complained through the Western Morning News in the winter of 1932 about men wearing this rig on the Parade Ground all day in the cold. Shame! Note: Two of these lads met up again last year, through the "Navy News"—the first time for over 50 years.

OUR SAILORS

1. - Physical drill

The 160-ton electrical revolving cantilever crane, built in 1909 and sited on the east side of the Prince of Wales Basin. Used mainly for removing guns, turrets and turbines from battleships. Last used in 1978 and now replaced by a 75 ton crane. (The ship is believed to be the *Centurion*).

A 15-in shell for 'Lizzies' big 'uns. (Weight one ton). Food for the Navy's big guns—thanks to the Department controlled by the Directors of Naval Ordnance.

Final full dress rehearsal for the march through London for the Coronation of HM King George VI in 1937. The column is shown moving towards St Levan's Gate, past Goschen Street, having marched half a mile—with another twelve to go. The officer in full dress was later promoted and appointed second in command of *HMS Orion*.

A sailor's farewell for Bobbie, who had been a member of staff at the R.N. Barracks, Devonport (see book 2, page 48) for many years and was paid off in 1937. He was replaced by a mare called Betty.

Horses served the Dockyard almost as long as people and their retirement in 1960 marked the end of 260 years service. These handsome animals are shown outside Albert Gate with their drivers, ready to be walked back through New Passage Hill and Durnford Street towards the stables under the Union Street Railway Arches.

Coaling Station. With the collier alongside the ship, and whilst her derricks are being topped, the party of coal bag fillers go at once into the hold to fill bags. The dusty scene is pictured here, a bundle of bags having just been lowered for a further filling. The ship being coaled was *HMS Australia*, circa 1910. With 31 boilers, a typical load of coal would be approximately 3,170 tons. Oil fuel stocks were generally low for the Navy and these coal burners could go on extensive 'Showing the Flag' cruises and patrols in the North Sea, with a range of 6,330 n. miles.

CHEER UP!
THINGS ARE NOT SO BLACK AS THEY LOOK

UNIFORMS

The foretop division being photographed on board *HMS Curlew*, whilst serving overseas on a China Station commission 1920-22. Shown here wearing straw hats, which were replaced in 1921 by white helmets.

A group of Royal Marine Police Special Reserves, in heavy serge greatcoats and winter gear, posing in front of one of the buildings at the RN Air Station, Roborough. During the War, aircrews were billetted at the George Hotel, and such aircraft as Sword Fish, Albacores and Gladiators used the runway, as did the RAF. Now Brymon Airways and the Royal Naval Chipmunk trainer aircraft from Britannia College use the modernised runways and facilities.

Air Radio Mechanic Wren Evans, in 1947, photographed by her father (a professional photographer) on her first weekend pass. The uniform is a navy serge WRNS jacket, standard bell-bottomed trousers and square-neck cotton top. The hat was a soft version of a sailor's hat, showing only 'HMS' and later in that year named bands were re-introduced. Wren Evans did basic training at Burghfield, near Reading, and served at Culdrose on Airborne Radar from 1948-49.

The author's father, QM Endacott, whilst serving at Dalditch Camp, wearing the new khaki 'Battle Dress' of rough serge which was buttoned up to the neck. The khaki field service cap was still in use until late 1943, when it was replaced by the blue beret. Eventually, in 1948, the smarter dress with open neck and tie was worn by all ranks.

INITIAL SEAMAN TRAINING

CPO Henry Williams teaching young cadet seamen the handling of the steering wheel and the use of the compass inside the binnacle on this simulator platform at The Bethel on the Barbican, in 1944. Incidentally the Bethel is now the Little Theatre.

Junior Seaman Nicholas Samuel of Plymouth is another 'Young Drake', having completed his basic training at the shore establishment HMS Raleigh in 1987. Standing proudly with his father—a serving CPO—they are both descendants of a sea-faring family, Nicholas's grandfather, great-grandfather and great-great-grandfather all having served in the Navy—as far back as the mid 1800's, on the Wooden Wallers.

HMS *Raleigh*. Her Majesty Queen Elizabeth the Queen Mother visiting the establishment in 1985. She is pictured here helping to stir the Christmas Pudding mixture with a helping of traditional Rum. During her visit the Queen Mother saw many departments and crew members undergoing training.

HMS *Raleigh*, the new-entry training establishment at Torpoint, claims to be the best equipped seamanship school in Western Europe. As well as sophisticated hi-tech ship work, the precise art of serving wine correctly is not being overlooked by these young Supply Stewards under training.

EDUCATIONAL HERITAGE

A is for Artificer
Who works down below
The engines obey him
And go fast or slow

B is for Battleship
Bristling with guns
She scours the seas
day and night
Searching for Huns

C is for Cruiser
A big ship indeed
With the guns of a Dreadnought
But much higher speed.

D is for Destroyer a very fast ship
A U-boat has hard work to give her the slip.

E is for Ensign,
the Flag of the free.
It is flown by all warships
in port or at sea.

F is for Furnace in the
stoke-hold below.
By stokers fed often
to keep it a-glow.

G is for Gunner
with sight very keen.
He throbs with delight
when the enemy's seen.

H is for Hammock —
the naval man's bed.
He sleeps like a top,
though men tramp overhead.

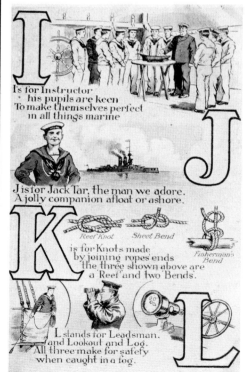

I is for Instructor
his pupils are keen
To make themselves perfect
in all things marine

J is for Jack Tar, the man we adore.
A jolly companion afloat or ashore.

Reef Knot   *Sheet Bend*   *Fisherman's Bend*

K is for Knots made
by joining ropes' ends
The three shown above are
a Reef and two Bends.

L stands for Leadsman.
and Lookout and Log.
All three make for safety
when caught in a fog.

K Is for Kitchen—but Field Kitchen working is what this young seaman is experiencing. He may be a member of a landing party some time during his career.

M is for Midshipman
fresh from the college
At Dartmouth where officers
youthful gain knowledge.

N is for Navigator, skilled in the art
Of finding the course of the
ship on the chart.

O is for Officer
men all obey.
And Bravo! for duty well done
he will say.

P stands for Paymaster
paying the crew.
His care is to see that each man
has his due.

Q is for Quarterdeck
always well swept
All ranks must salute it
a custom well kept

R is for Rudder
the ship must obey
No course can be
followed
if this is away

S is for Signal
a sailor can read.
T is for Telegraph
pointing 'Full Speed'.

U is for Uniform
Blue, with Gold Lace
By the bands on his cuff
A man's rank you can trace.

Captain   Lieutenant

V is for "Victory", that
'old wooden wall'.
The great Nelson's
Flagship, so
treasured by all.

W is for Warships which
guard us night and day.

But

XYZ
can't help us
so there's nothing more to say.

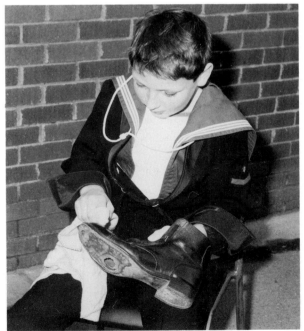

S is for Shine—but the uppers should never be over worked on without constant inspection of the underside, where the wet really penetrates.

CADET CORPS

While visiting HMS *Raleigh* in 1985, Her Majesty Queen Elizabeth the Queen Mother inspects some of the naval personnel of the future—the Sea Cadet Corps.

Girls Nautical Training Corps performing the Ceremony of the Colours in the Drill Hall, HMS Drake, in July 1979, just prior to the 1980 amalgamation with the Sea Cadet Corps.

The Royal Marines Volunteer Cadet Corps, outside the 'Long Room', Stonehouse, Plymouth in 1983. Formed in 1903 for the sons of the Plymouth Div. RM Light Infantry. In 1977 girls were allowed in to take part in the full range of work. Many go on to join bands of the Regular Army and Royal Marines. The Plymouth unit is the largest of the four groups in the country.

TRANSFER AT SEA

Here we see a man being transferred by light jackstay from ship to ship, using the RAS highpoint system.

Another modern method of transferring personnel is by a support sling on the end of a winch wire below a helicopter. All Air/Sea Rescue work is carried out this way, with the addition of a stretcher cage for the injured.

PASSING THRO' TIME

HMS Ulster. Her first association with Devonport was in September, 1943, and for the next thirty-seven years she was to be seen in and around the Port and was last used as the static Harbour Training Ship for HMS Raleigh. She is pictured here leaving Plymouth during October 1980, bound for the breakers' yard at Inverkeithing, assisted by the paddle tug *Favourite*, who in turn made the one-way journey in April 1983 to become a target for the Royal Navy in Gibraltar.

This apparatus was used in the Devonport Dockyard to give steam heating to vessels undergoing refits, and was known as a Donkey Boiler. Steam could be raised to 120lb/sq.in., the centre unit was the cab area for the crew and the end unit a water tank. With all dockside services now built into subway service tunnels and connected to the ship, this outfit is now obsolete.

A Gannet all-weather early warning aircraft returning to a Carrier, her arrester hook approaching the raised wire. Gannets were fitted with contra-rotating propellers, and powerful search radar. Sadly, these aircraft were phased out in 1978 with the introduction of the helicopter and the demise soon after of the large Aircraft Carriers.

The WASP helicopter first appeared in the Royal Navy during 1961 and carried homing torpedoes and, later, A/S missiles to increase the ship's own weapon range. In 1977 the more highly sophisticated LYNX was brought into service, but Wasps continue to be used by the Fleet and are shown here returning to the flight deck of the frigate *Arethusa*. Sadly the final flight of these small but versatile machines will be during 1988—they will be greatly missed.

GUNS

The presence of the Royal Navy battleships with their large guns at high elevation was all that was needed to show we were ready to defend the British Empire and its people. Sadly the Empire has been greatly reduced, and with it the great guns.

Since the last War technology has taken a great stride forward and now smaller ships, with sophisticated missile systems, are the new arm of the Navy.

HMS Roberts, Monitor, of 7,970 tons, launched 1942, arrived at Devonport after active service during the war. She was to be used in a variety of roles for the next twenty years and is shown here at her moorings opposite Bull Point, from where she left for Inverkeithing and the breakers' yard in 1965. At that time she was the last ship in the Royal Navy to mount 15-inch guns.

HMS Orion, a Leander class cruiser built at Devonport and completed in 1933. She took part in many wartime operations, including bombardment support during the D-Day landings. After the end of the war and a period in reserve, she was used for underwater trials, following which she was sold to Arnott Young and broken up at Troon in 1949.

This Twin 4.5″ Gun Turret was removed from one of the early Batch I Leanders in 1973 and replaced by the IKARA A/S missile system. Gradually all the Leanders' gun turrets have disappeared in favour of Exocet or Sea Wolf Missile Systems (see page 52 bottom). Most frigates and destroyers are now being built with only a single 4.5″ gun plus many missile systems.

HMS *Cambridge*, Wembury, the Navy's Gunnery School since 1956, provides live firing practice for officers and ratings over a firing range extending 13 miles out to sea. Here we can see the 4.5" Mark 8 Gun mounted in front of the New Leach Building. This gun is now fitted on Type 21's, 22's and 42's.

Trainees also receive instruction in firing close-range anti-aircraft guns, as shown here, and in maintenance work. About 200 permanent staff train over 4,000 students every year at this establishment.

Gradually gun weapon systems have, with the advent of high technology, in the main been replaced by Guided Missile systems as shown here on *HMS Arethusa*. The twin 4.5" gun turret normally forward of the bridge (see page 51 bottom) has been replaced by the IKARA weapon, a rocket-propelled anti-submarine missile.

NAVAL COLLEGES

Here a young officer is using a planimeter to aid his work on the Sheer Drawing of a ship in the Keyham College classroom. During the early 1950's the Dockyard took over the college building and it became known as the Devonport Dockyard Technical College. It had the capacity to accommodate 1,500 apprentices and its high standard of teaching could lead to a Cadetship in the Royal Corps of Naval Constructors or a career as an Electrical Officer.

R.N.E.C. *Keyham* (see Book 2, page 33). After 105 years of naval training and accommodation, the College is being removed from its site by a modern-day excavator and teams of lorries. Some principal items have been transferred to Manadon as a reminder of great traditions, but the skyline will never be the same.

The Royal Naval Engineering College, *Manadon* is the establishment for the technical training of engineer officers, whose responsibilities will be for nuclear submarines, aircraft and ships with High Tech weapon systems. Partial transfer was made from Keyham in 1940 and developed in stages until the final accommodation building and Great Hall were opened in 1958 by the Duke of Edinburgh.

A model of a gun turret being eagerly examined by Engineer Officers at the Manadon College site. At the time this was one of many newly-introduced training facilities to be installed to increase the syllabus of the student.

Engineer Officers working at Manadon College in one of the workshops on a Seafire Type 46 engine assembly.

These illustrations show the changes to the Midshipman's uniform from the wooden wall period of 1808 to the steel dreadnought and battleship period of the 1930's.

Passing out day at *Britannia* Royal Naval College, watched by proud families. It is a very important day to the participants, who have completed a comprehensive course to develop officer qualities and acquire a wide foundation of professional knowledge. As many as 35 countries are represented, giving an indication of the universal high regard for the College and its training.

A Naval Officer and WRNS Officer Cadet on the parade ground of the College. The former would be expected to attend a full Course of 56 weeks whilst the WRNS underwent only 14 weeks. Wren Officer training was not introduced until 1976.

The Naval College towering over houses and moorings on the River Dart. The warship P262 is the patrol boat *Peterel*, used by the college as the Dartmouth Navigational Training Ship, along with motor picket boats and ocean-going yachts, giving the best possible varied sea experiences.

THE FLEET AIR ARM

Very early on a Sunday morning in November 1983 the Helston road was closed to allow this Sea Vixen and its companion to be towed from Culdrose to the Flambards Aero Park. These aircraft were added to the outdoor display at this Theme Park.

HM Coastguard is responsible for co-ordinating all civil and marine search and rescue operations around the UK coastline. Here a Wessex helicopter from Culdrose is hovering over the scene of a cliff rescue, with the RNLI lifeboat standing off to give additional assistance if required.

Constable Curnow with his police dog 'Prince' at Culdrose in the early 1960's, in front of a Bedford Admiralty Police Van. During his long career he became the C.I.D Officer and retired at the age of 65 in 1971, having received the Queen's Police Long Service and Good Conduct Medal.

HRH Prince Andrew joined Culdrose in 1980 and completed a training course on the Gazelle helicopter to receive his Wings. He then progressed his training with Seakings of the 706 Squadron, and went with the 820 Squadron on front line duty to the Falklands in 1981.

A Wessex V Helicopter from Culdrose comes to the aid of the yacht *Camargue* during the 1979 Fastnet Race. The Culdrose crews flew over 200 hours over 3 days and winched 73 survivors to safety from a fleet of dis-masted and derelict yachts caught in a sudden storm between Lands End and the Irish Coast.

The entire unit of helicopters and complete back-up outfits which go into stand-by alert when S & R situations occur. Local hospitals, both RN and civilian, also go on alert until the situation is assessed and dealt with, and eventually stand-down is issued.

A 'flock of wrens' gathered around a Sea King Mk 5 at RNAS *Culdrose*. Each Wren is portraying a different role to show the diversified range of skills—Air Engineering Mechanic; MT Driver; PT Instructor; Radio Operator; Training Support Assistant; Writer Gen. & Pay; Photographer; Dental Hygienist; Education; Telephonist; Quarters Assistant; Nurse; Met Observer; Cook; Steward; Radar Plotter and Stores Assistant—a team not to be trifled with.

THE ROYAL FLEET AUXILIARY SERVICE

The long range escort destroyer *Wanderer* in 1943, carrying out the replenishment-at-sea (RAS) operation in the line astern position from a fleet oiler during a North Atlantic Convoy exercise. She was built at Fairfields in 1919 and converted to long-range work at Devonport in 1943. Eventually sold to British Iron & Steel Company for breaking up and then to Hughes Bolckow of Durham in 1946.

The support tanker *RFA Orangeleaf* carrying out an abreast ''RAS'' operation in 1962, replenishing the aircraft carrier *HMS Victorious* with fuel and stores. *Orangeleaf* is one of six Leaf Class vessels of approximate full load displacement of 37,700 tonnes and is part of the Royal Fleet Auxiliary Service armada of 29 ships which are manned by civilian personnel.

A 'RAS' operation taking place during a NATO exercise directed from Devonport. The ships involved were the US Destroyer *O'Bannon*, the British RFA *Grey Rover* and the German Destroyer *Luetjens*.

Olna leaving Devonport, aided by tugs off Mount Wise. She is one of a class of three large fleet tankers known as the OL Class. These tankers are capable of replenishing three ships simultaneously (one either side and one astern) and each carry two helicopters. With their strengthened hulls they can operate in ice, and generally carry FFO, Diesels, Luboil, Avcat, Mogas and dry stores.

OPERATION CORPORATE

This commercial container ship had her hatches covered and a flight deck constructed with securing eyeplates to lash down aircraft. A hangar was added, plus a high ramp from the helicopter deck to the stowage areas below. The Dockyard worked night and day to piece together this Commercial Armada for the Falklands conflict.

The Logistic group of the Royal Marines assembling at Stonehouse Barracks, en route to the South Atlantic as part of the Falkland Islands Task Force in 1982.

The *Atlantic Conveyor* was the first Cunard merchant ship to be converted to an instant aircraft carrier at Devonport. She is seen here in Plymouth Sound, taking on one of the Sea Harriers. Sadly, during the campaign she was hit by an Exocet missile, gutted by fire and subsequently abandoned. Most of the helicopters were destroyed but the Harriers had flown clear earlier.

The Royal Marines—ever conscious that fitness and alertness can save a life—are being put through a series of exercises on the flight deck during the 8,000 mile voyage to the Falklands.

HMS Arrow, escorted by tugs, returning from her ordeal in the Falklands to receive a welcome home reception from the Mount Wise area. She was the first ship to be attacked, and incurred only one casualty—a wounded AB. During her three-month spell of duty she steamed 30,000 miles, her men, engines and weapons continuously on call.

With these glances at the Navy and its many branches, the supportive Dockyard and its widely experienced workforce it is hoped that you, the reader, have now a fuller picture of our 'Naval Heritage'.

Please give these combined forces your support annually at the traditional Navy Days where you can ''See the Ships and Meet the Men and Women''.